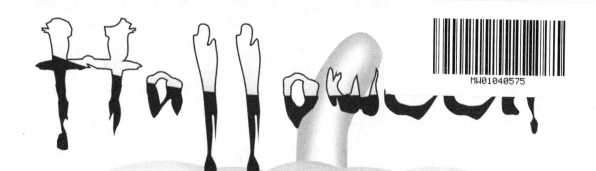

Halloween

I Spy

BELONGS TO

....

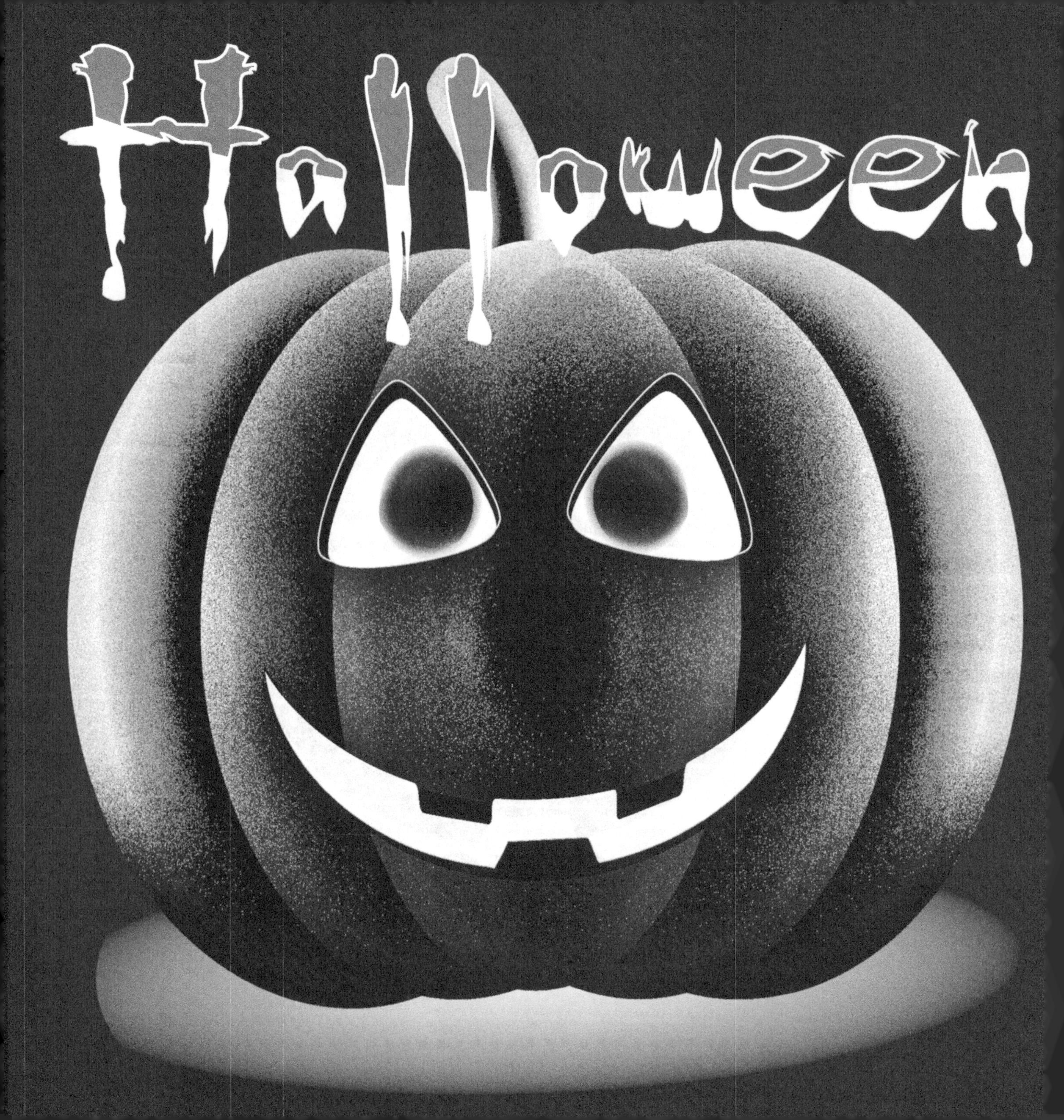
Halloween

Halloween

Halloween

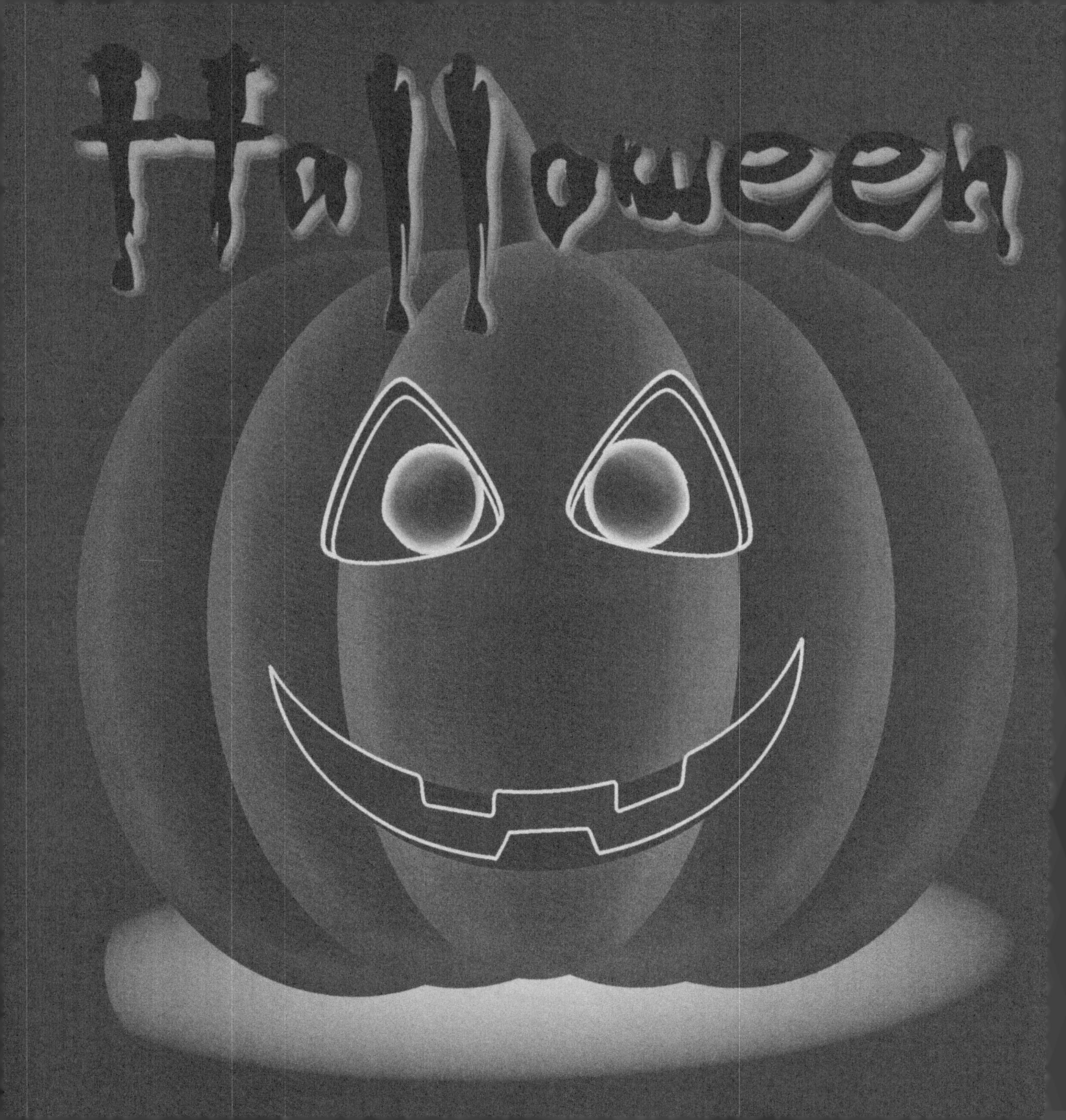
Halloween

Halloween

Halloween

Halloween

Halloween

Halloween

Halloween

Halloween

Halloween

Halloween

Halloween

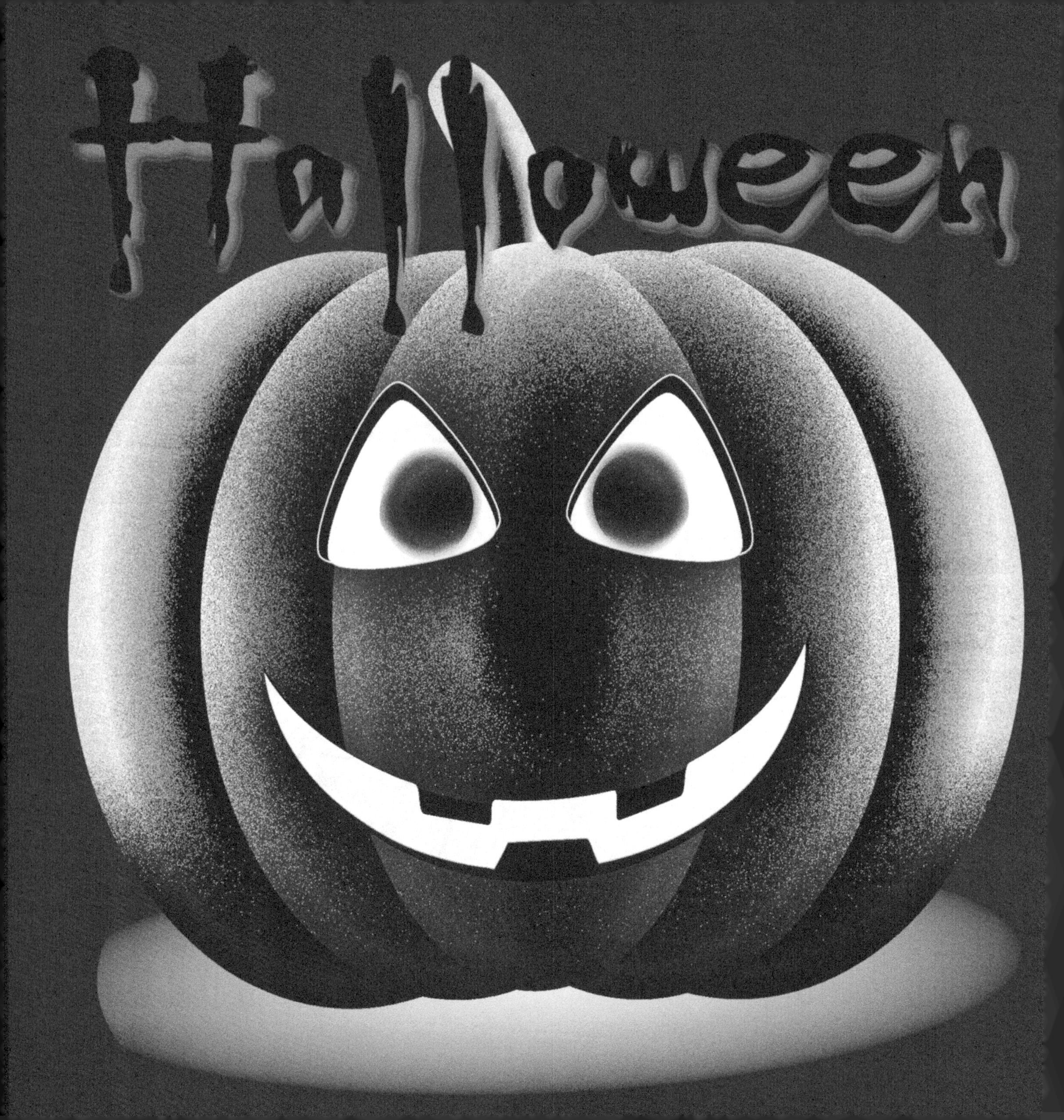
Halloween

Halloween

Halloween

Halloween

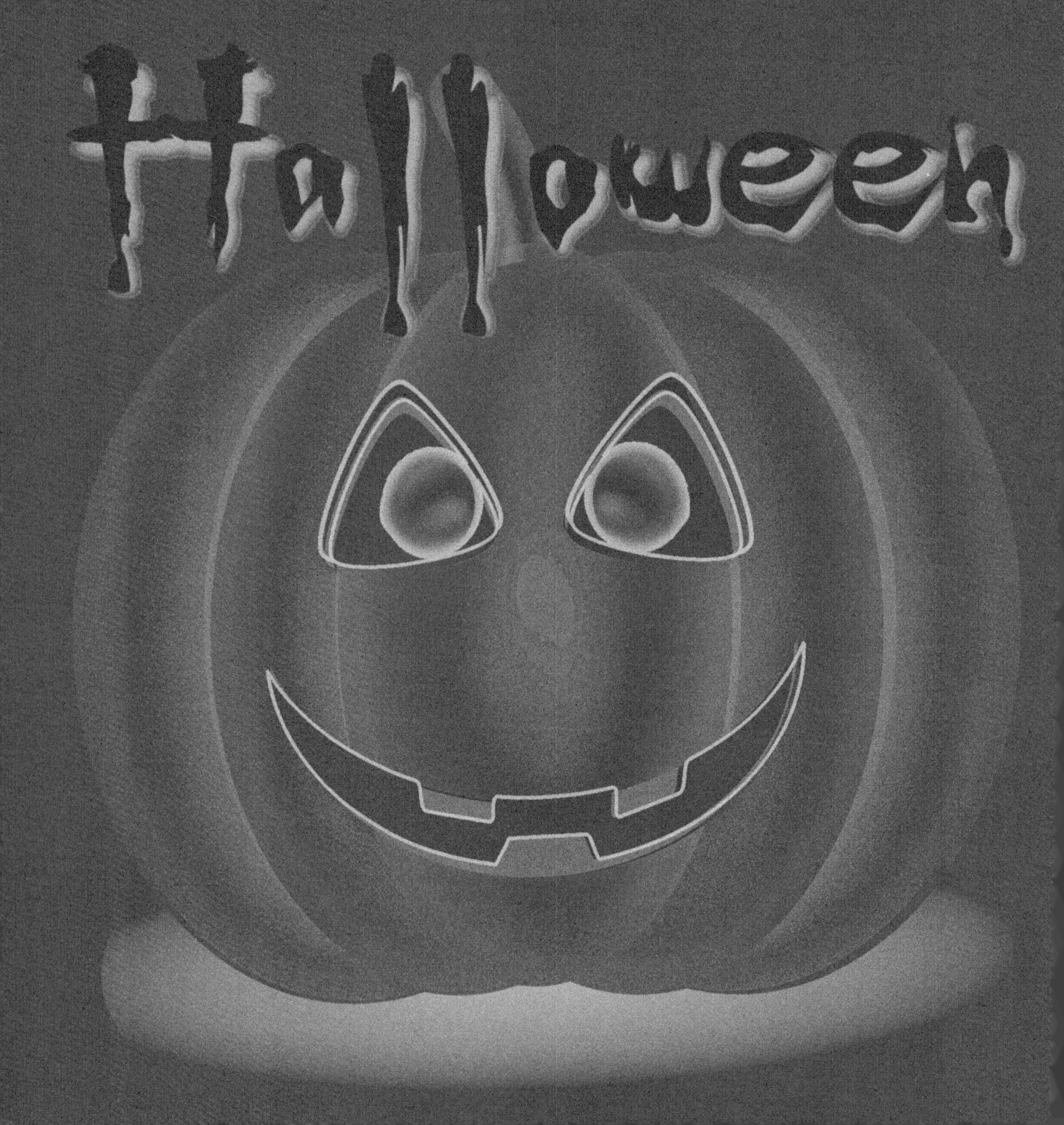
Halloween

Halloween

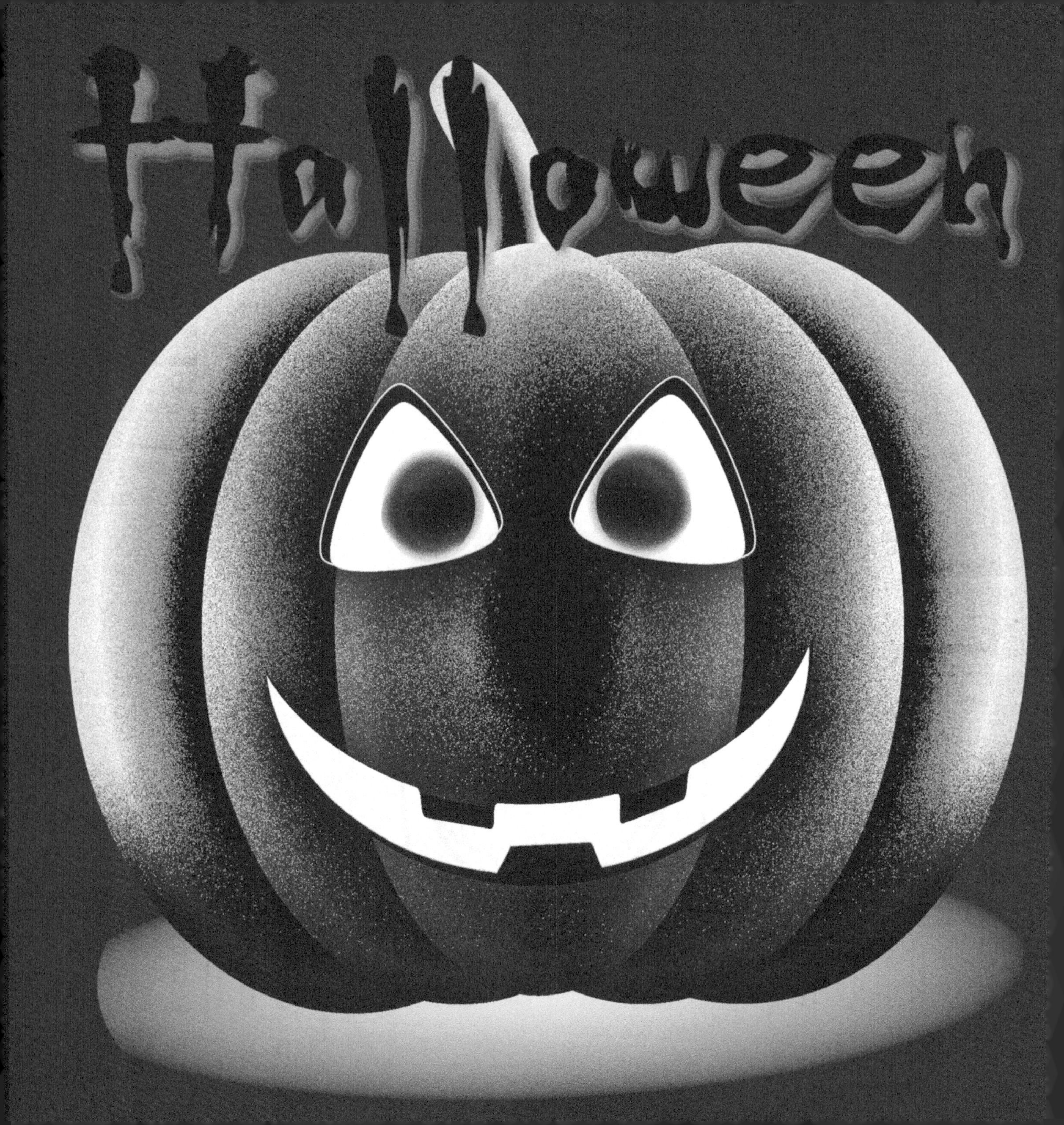
Halloween

Halloween

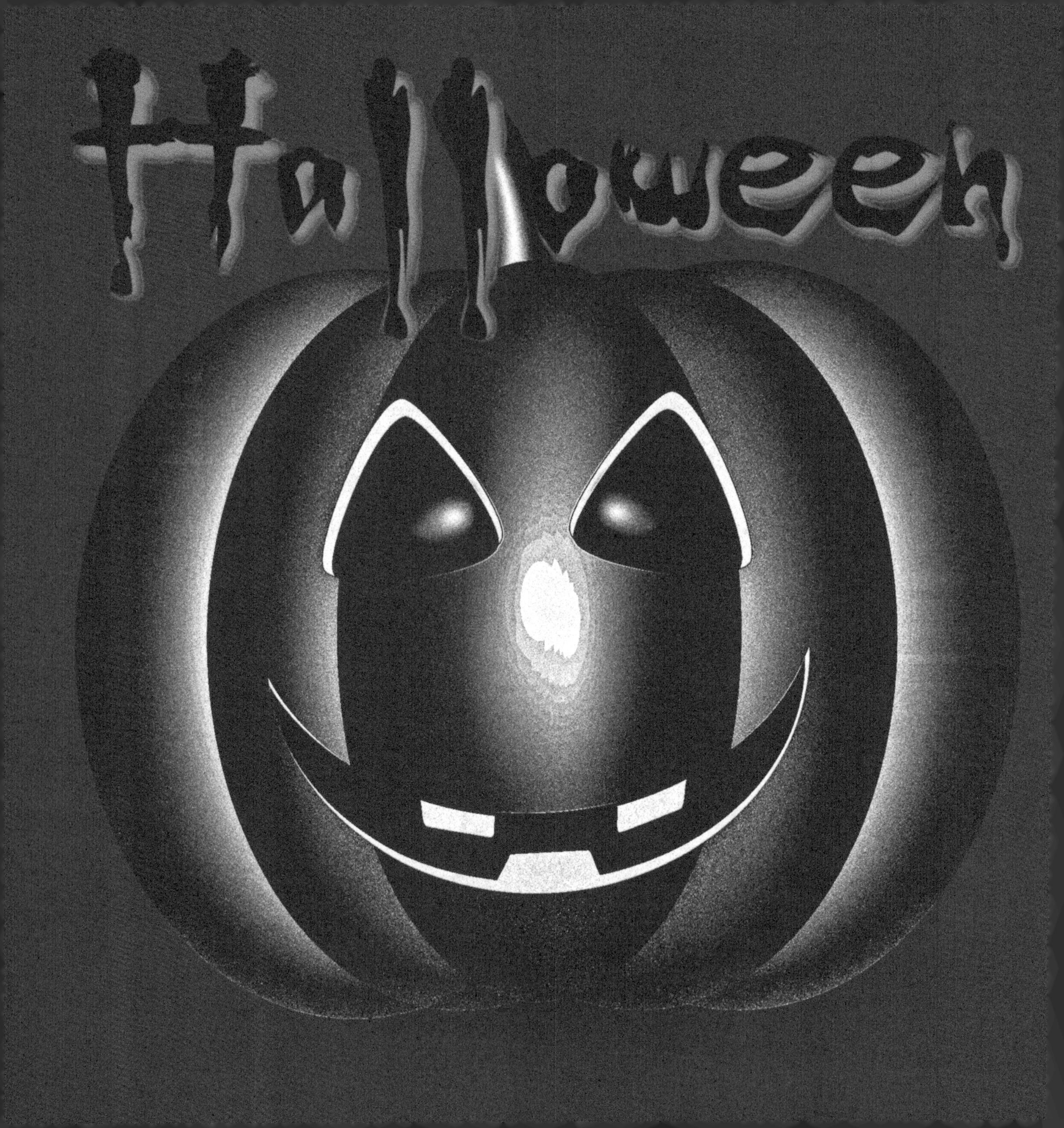
Halloween

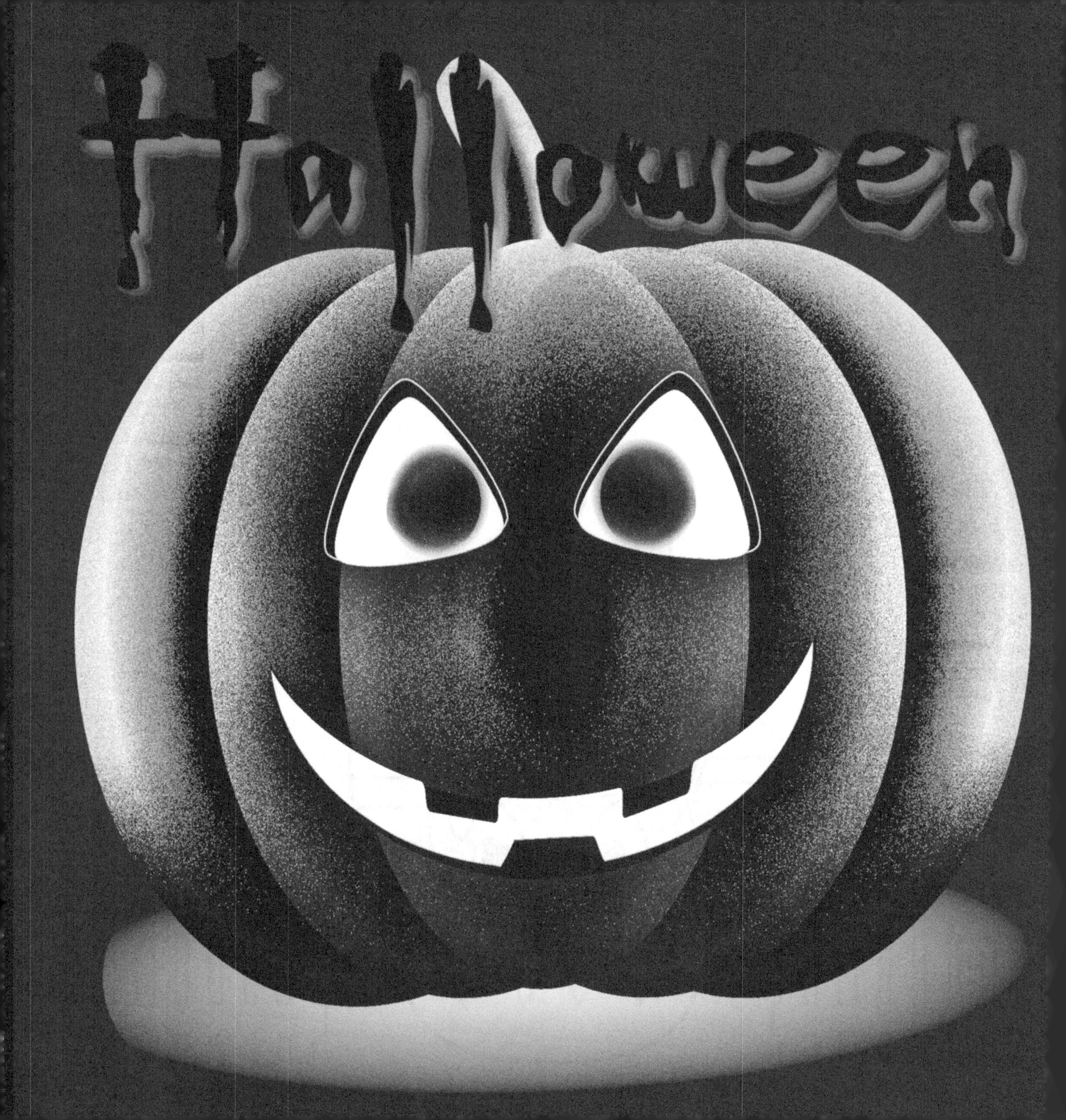
Halloween

Halloween

Halloween

Halloween

Halloween

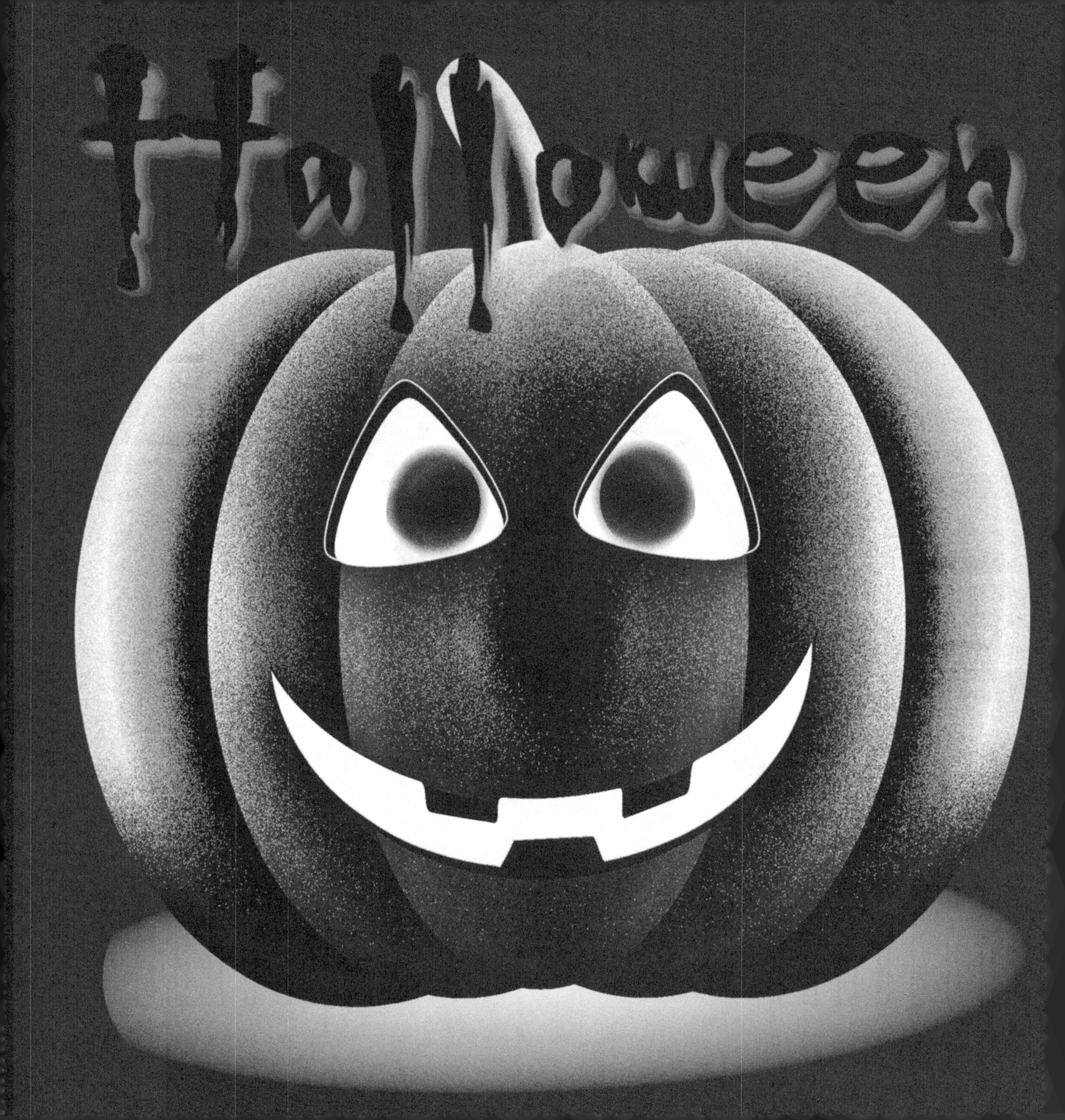
Halloween

Halloween

Thank You For Buying
This

Halloween Coloring Book
For Kids

Stay Whis Us and See
The Next Editions
HALLOWEEN
COLOR ME

Made in United States
North Haven, CT
08 October 2023